CW01371083

Consolations

LINDA KELLY is the distinguished author of a dozen books on late eighteenth and early nineteenth century literary and political history, including *The Young Romantics* and *Susanna, the Captain & the Castrato* published by Starhaven. Her husband is the writer Laurence Kelly; they live in London and have three children.

Consolations

A Commonplace Book

Linda Kelly

Starhaven

to Chip

©Linda Kelly 2017
ISBN 0-936315-42-3

STARHAVEN, 42 Frognal, London NW3 6AG
books@starhaven.org.uk
www.starhaven.org.uk
+44 (0)7957 346878

Typeset in Minion by John Mallinson
Printed by CPI, 38 Ballard's Lane, London N3 2BJ

This is one of an initial edition of 100 copies for family, friends and a happy few.

Consolations

Shortly after I got married, more than half a century ago, my mother-in-law presented me with a beautiful red leather album. Its pristine gilt-edged pages seemed too precious to fill with anything so prosaic as recipes or addresses. I decided to use it as a commonplace book and have been keeping it, off and on, ever since. The collection has always been for my own consumption but recently I lent it to one of my daughters who was suffering from depression and she found it so comforting that I thought it might be a source of consolation – or interest or amusement – for others too. There is no rhyme or reason for my choices except that, as with all proper commonplace books, I have never set out to look for them. They have always sprung up naturally from what I was reading, the only criterion being that I felt impelled to stop and write them down. As I am very lazy – one of my recurring themes is the difficulty of getting down to work – this is surely the supreme test.

At first I thought I might rearrange the collection into categories – London, for instance, has been another recurring theme – but in the end I decided to let it form its own pattern and, apart from cutting it a little, have left it in the order it was written. The sources, often rather sketchy, are as noted at the time.

Inevitably one's outlook changes over the years. The first entries tend to be more lyrical, the later perhaps more reflective. Some of them may seem over familiar, but they came to me fresh when I first read them, and I saw no point in leaving them out because they were well known. Occasionally I've come across the same quotation in another collection afterwards. I was thrilled, for instance, to see that W. H. Auden had chosen the same passage as I had from a Sherlock Holmes short story in his anthology, *A Certain World*. But though I love anthologies I've avoided quoting from those of other people; it somehow seemed a form of cheating. (Collections of poetry like *The Oxford Book of English Verse* are exceptions to this unwritten rule.) I have also avoided quoting from Shakespeare; he is such a world in himself that there would have been no room for anyone else once I began.

The red leather album is falling to pieces now, another good reason for gathering up its contents before it collapses altogether. There are still a few more pages to fill and I hope to go on making fresh discoveries –

> The soul's dark cottage, battered and decayed,
> Lets in new light through chinks that time has made.

But this is where I've got so far.

Down by the Salley Gardens

Down by the salley gardens my love and I did meet,
She passed the salley gardens with little snow-white feet.
She bid me take love easy, as the leaves grow on the tree
But I, being young and foolish, with her would not agree.

In a field by the river my love and I did stand
And on my leaning shoulder she laid her snow-white hand.
She bid me take life easy, as the grass grows on the weirs,
But I was young and foolish, and now am full of tears.

W. B. Yeats

So, we'll go no more a-roving
    So late into the night,
Though the heart be still as loving
    And the moon be still as bright.

For the sword outwears its sheath,
    And the heart wears out the breast,
And the heart must pause to breathe
    And love itself have rest.

Though the night was made for loving
    And the day returns too soon,
Yet we'll go no more a-roving
    By the light of the moon.

Lord Byron to Tom Moore, following the Venice Carnival

The Visitor

He comes with Western winds, with evening's wandering airs,
With that clear dusk of heaven that brings the thickest stars;
Winds take a pensive tone, and stars a tender fire
And visions rise and change which kill me with desire -

Desire for nothing known in my maturer years,
When joy grew mad with awe at counting future tears:
When, if my spirit's sky was full of flashes warm,
I knew not whence they came, from sun or thunderstorm.

But first a hush of peace – a soundless calm descends;
The struggle of distress and fierce impatience ends;
Mute music soothes my breast – unuttered harmony
That I could never dream till earth was lost to me.

Then dawns the Invisible, the unseen its truth reveals;
My outward sense is gone, my inward essence feels –
Its wings are almost free, its home, its harbour found;
Measuring the gulf it stoops and dares the final bound!

Oh dreadful is the check, intense the agony
When the ear begins to hear and the eye begins to see;
When the pulse begins to throb, the brain to think again,
The soul to feel the flesh, and the flesh to feel the chain!

Yet I would lose no sting, would wish no torture less;
The more that anguish racks the earlier it will bless;

And robed in fires of hell or bright with heavenly shine,
If it but herald death, the vision is divine.

>   Emily Brontë

∞

>   Here shadows lie
>   Whilst earth is sadd,
>   Still hopes to die
>   To him she hadd.
>   In bliss is hee
>   Whom I loved best
>   Thrice happy shee
>   With him to rest.
>   So shall I bee
>   With him I loved
>   And he with mee
>   And both us blessed.
>   Love made me poet
>   And this I writt;
>   My heart did do it
>   And not my wit.

Composed by the wife of Lord Justice Tanfield (died 1625) and engraved on their joint monument at Burford in Oxfordshire.

∞

The Flower

How fresh, O Lord, how sweet and clean
Are thy returns! ev'n as the flowers in spring,
To which, besides their own demean,
The late-past frosts tributes of pleasure bring.
    Grief melts away
    Like snow in May,
As if there were no such cold thing.

Who would have thought my shrivel'd heart
Could have recovered greennesse? It was gone
Quite underground, as flowers depart
To see their mother-root, when they have blown,
    Where they together
    All the hard weather
Dead to the world, keep house unknown …

And now in age I bud again
After so many deaths I live and write;
I once more smell the dew and rain,
And relish versing. O, my only light
    It cannot be
    That I am he
On whom thy tempests fell all night.

These are thy wonders, Lord of love,
That make us see we are but flowers that glide;
Which when we once can finde and prove,
Thou hast a garden for us where to bide.

> Who would be more,
> Swelling through store,
> Forfeit their Paradise by their pride.
>
> George Herbert

∞

> The truth cannot impose itself except by virtue of its own truth, and it makes its entry into the mind at once quietly and with power.
>
> *Dignitatis Humanae*, Second Vatican Council, 1966

∞

> … The days passed slowly, one by one,
> I fed the ducks, reproved my wife,
> Played Handel's Largo on the fife
> Or gave the dog a run.
>
> Harry Graham, quoted in Agatha Christie's *The Hollow*

∞

> Waking at times in the night she found assurance
> In his regular breathing but wondered whether
>   It was really worth it and where
>   The river had flowed away
>   And where were the white flowers.
>
> Louis MacNeice, 'Les Sylphides'

∞

Night

The sun descending in the west
The evening star does shine;
The birds are silent in their nest,
And I must seek for mine.
The moon like a flower,
In heaven's high bower,
With silent delight
Sits and smiles on the night.

Farewell, green fields and happy grove
Where flocks have took delight
Where lambs have nibbled, silent move
The feet of angels bright;
Unseen they pour blessing
And joy without ceasing,
On each bird and blossom
And each sleeping bosom.

They look in every thoughtless nest
Where birds are cover'd warm;
They visit caves of every beast
To keep them all from harm.
If they see any weeping
That should have been sleeping
They pour sleep on their head
And sit down by their bed.

Where wolves and tygers howl for prey,
They pitying stand and weep;

Seeking to drive their thirst away,
And keep them from the sheep.
But, if they rush dreadful,
The angels, most heedful,
Receive each mild spirit,
New worlds to inherit.

And there the lion's ruddy eyes
Shall flow with tears of gold
And pitying the tender cries,
And walking round his fold,
Saying: Wrath by his meekness
And by his health, sickness
Are driven away
From our immortal day.

And now beside thee, bleating lamb
I can lie down and sleep;
And think on him who bore thy name,
Graze after thee and weep.
For, washed in life's river,
My bright mane for ever
Shall shine like the gold,
As I guard o'er the fold.

William Blake

∞

What if some little paine the passage have
That makes fraile flesh to fear the bitter wave?
Is not short paine well borne, that brings long ease,

And layes the soul to sleep in quiet grave?
Sleepe after toyle, port after stormie seas
Ease after war, death after life, does greatly please.

Edmund Spenser, *The Faerie Queen*

∞

Though the practice of his art may afford a writer his chief pleasure, no less than his principal and constant source of worry, though too, a sudden inspiration may constitute his greatest luxury, yet a minute account of this, his real existence, would be – could only be – of slight interest to the reader. How is it possible to picture for him the quotidian miseries and splendours of a life attached to an inkpot, the many months spent at a table, the hours when every disturbance is furiously resented, the other, more occasional moments when every interruption is welcome, the evenings when an author looks on his work and finds it good, or those frequent nights when it seems to him to have fallen unbelievably short of what he had intended, the inflations of self conceit and the agonies of self reproach, the days when everything grows to giant proportions because it has meaning, and the afternoons when all dwindles to pygmy and shows none?

Osbert Sitwell, *Laughter in the Next Room*

∞

Between cockcrow and matins bell
In a cool room of light and air
In a cool house beside the Vare
My mother knew my father well
And I was well begotten there.

The church bells call across the plain
'Come people to your prayers again'.
The sun above the stable crept
And bird began to call to bird.
Within the house the servants stirred.
My father and my mother slept.

O happy sleep, O happy love
I see you as the years go by
United still in constancy
Warm hearted each to each and proof
Against the world's malicious eye.
Within that household calm and sage
I crawled and stumbled, walked and ran
Up the long stairs that lead to man
Until at last I reached the age
Of indiscretion and began
My own unaided pilgrimage.

Ronald McNair Scott

Memory Test†

This monarch was sincere, open, gallant, liberal, intrepid, zealous, inflexible and courageous but with these virtues he combined the vices of violence, cruelty, profusion, rapacity, injustice, obstinacy, arrogance, bigotry, presumption and caprice.

† The test is to recite it by heart after looking at it once.

∞

Victor Hugo

Victor in Drama, Victor in Romance,
Cloud-weaver of phantasmal hopes and fears,
French of the French, and Lord of human tears;
Child-lover; Bard whose fame-lit laurels glance,
Darkening the wreaths of all that would advance
Beyond our strait, their claim to be thy peers …

Alfred, Lord Tennyson

∞

Circumstances determine our lives but we shape our lives by what we make of circumstances.

Lewis Namier, re. Sir John Wheeler Bennett

∞

… Hommes durs! Vie atroce et laide d'ici bas!

Ah! que du moins, loin des baisers et des combats
Quelque chose demeure un peu sur la montagne,
Quelque chose du coeur enfantin et subtil,
Bonté, respect! Car, qu'est-ce qui nous accompagne,
Et vraiment, quand la mort viendra, que reste-t-il?

Paul Verlaine, 'Sagesse'

∞

Hogg and half of these Scotch and Lake troubadours are spoilt by living in little circles and petty societies. London and the world is the only place to take the conceit out of a man.

Byron to Tom Moore, 3 August 1814

∞

> This life is a city of crooked streets
> Death is the market-place where all men meet.
> If life were merchandise that money could buy
> The rich would live and the poor would die.

Verses on a tombstone, quoted in M. K. Ashby's *Joseph Ashby of Tysoe, 1859-1919*

∞

If I were young and handsome as I was, instead of old and faded as I am, and you could lay the empire of the world at my feet, you should never share the heart and hand that once belonged to John, Duke of Marlborough.

The Duchess of Marlborough, refusing a proposal from the Duke of Somerset

∞

The falsities of an alienated social reality are rejected in the favour of an upward psychopathic mobility to the point of divinity, each one of us a Christ – but with none of the inconveniences of undertaking to intercede, of being a sacrifice, of reasoning with rabbis, of making sermons, of having disciples, of going to weddings and to funerals, of beginning something and at a certain point remarking that it is finished.

Lionel Trilling, *Sincerity and Authenticity*, re the New Age movement of the 1960s. (My editor takes issue with Trilling's characterization, but I shall let it stand.)

∞

Oh Lord God, when thou givest to thy servants to endeavour any great matter, grant us also to know that it is not the beginning, but the continuing of the same unto the end, until it be thoroughly finished, which yieldeth the true glory; through him who for the finishing of thy work laid down his life, our Redeemer, Jesus Christ.

Sir Francis Drake

The mystery of times past continually enthralls me. Here, long before us, dwelt folk as real as we are today, now utterly vanished, as we in turn shall vanish. History can miraculously restore them to our vision and understanding, can tell us a little of what were their hopes and fears, their words and works.

G. M. Trevelyan, quoted in *The Times*, 14 February 1976

The Maid Servant at the Inn

'It's queer,' she said, 'I see the light
As plain as I beheld it then,
All silver-like and calm and bright –
We've not had stars like that again!

'And she was such a gentle thing
To birth a baby in the cold.
The barn was dark and frightening –
This new one's better than the old.

'I mind my eyes were full of tears
For I was young and quick distressed,
But she was less than me in years
That held a son against her breast.

'I never saw a sweeter child –
The little one, the darling one! –
I mind I told her, when he smiled
You'd know he was his mother's son.

'It's queer that I should see them so –
The time they came to Bethlehem
Was more than thirty years ago;
I've prayed that all is well with them.'

Dorothy Parker

I know how you feel. I lost my little niece years ago, nursing her mostly myself, and cannot think of it even now without a tight feeling at the heart. It seems a terrible waste; and yet now I do believe it does not matter any more than it matters whether the drops of water in the river are out in the sunshine or swallowed down in the current below: all are moving to whatever is our mysterious goal – of that I feel more and more sure.

Freya Stark, letter to a friend who had just lost a nephew

Be regular and ordinary in your life, like a bourgeois, so that you can be violent and original in your books.

Gustave Flaubert

I never knew dying is so easy … I die without any feeling or hatred … never forget that life is nothing but a growing in love and a preparation for eternity.

Christoph Probst, writing to his sister before his execution for dropping anti-Hitler pamphlets in Munich University, 1943

∞

Then, said he, I am going to my Father's, and though with great difficulty I am got hither, yet now I do not repent all the trouble I have been at to arrive where I am. My sword I give to him that shall succeed me in my pilgrimage, and my courage and skill to him that can get it. My marks and scars I carry with me, to be a witness for me that I have fought his battles who now will be my rewarder. When the day that he must go hence was come many accompanied him to the riverside, into which as he went, he said, 'Death, where is thy sting?' And as he went down deeper, he said, 'Grave, where is thy victory?' So he passed over and all the trumpets sounded for him on the other side.

John Bunyan, *Pilgrim's Progress*

∞

La nuance de mépris de ceux qui vivent, pour ceux qui les regardent vivre.

Michel Déon, *Un Taxi Mauve* (about writers)

Work first, inspiration afterwards.

Igor Stravinsky

London horrified him and frightened him, it was so much beyond anything he could have imagined before seeing it… Ultimately, what most impressed itself upon Kenneth in the course of these wanderings was the unending persistence and size of the social effort that was demanded of a people, any people, by their history … Here in London he saw that hundreds of years could pass and still the moral and physical effort towards community had to be made. One could not plead exhaustion; one could not plead the achievements of the past; one could not even point to the grave yards and bomb sites and plead the futility of all effort; still less could one look to the future and look for ease there. The past and the present were intermingled inextricably in London because the present could neither free itself from the past nor rest on it, and what was true of London was true of any place where people lived, and what was true of Kenneth's time was true of any possible future.

Dan Jacobson, *The Evidence of Love*

So Good Luck came, and on my roof did light
Like noiseless snow; or as the dew of night:
Not all at once, but gently, as the trees
Are, by the sunbeams, tickled by degrees…

> Robert Herrick, 'The Coming of Good Luck'

∞

And what if the patient, whose sores you are washing, does not at once show you how grateful he is to you, but on the contrary, begins to torment you with his whims without noticing you or valuing your kindly services? What if he should start shouting at you, demanding something from you rudely (as often happens when people are in great pain) – what then? Will you still go on loving him?

> Dostoyevsky, *The Brothers Karamazov*

∞

In a drear-nighted December

In a drear-nighted December,
Too happy, happy tree,
Thy branches ne'er remember
Their green felicity:
The north cannot undo them
With a sleety whistle through them;
Nor frozen thawings glue them
From budding at the prime.

In a drear-nighted December
Too happy, happy brook,
Thy bubblings ne'er remember
Apollo's summer look;
But with a sweet forgetting
They stay their crystal fretting
Never, never petting
About the frozen time.

Ah! would 'twere so with many
A gentle girl and boy!
But were there ever any
Writhed not at past joy?
The feel of not to feel it,
When there is none to heal it,
Nor numbed sense to steal it,
Was never told in rhyme.

> John Keats, December 1817

I deprecate, however, in the strongest way, the attempts which have been made lately to get at and destroy these papers. The source of these outrages is known and if they are repeated I have Mr Holmes' authority for saying that the whole story concerning the politician, the light house owner and the cormorant will be given to the public. There is at least one reader who will understand.

> Arthur Conan Doyle, 'The Adventure of the Veiled Lodger'

Travail immédiat, même mauvais, vaut mieux que la rêverie.

      Charles Baudelaire, quoted by Gwen John

It would be difficult to speak adequately of London. It is not a pleasant place; it is not agreeable, or cheerful, or easy, or exempt from reproach. It is only magnificent. You can draw up a tremendous list of reasons why it should be insupportable. The fogs, the smoke, the dirt, the darkness, the wet, the distances, the brutal size of the place, the horrible numerosity of society, the manner in which this senseless bigness is fatal to amenity, to convenience, to conversation, to good manners – all this and much more you may expatiate on. You may call it dreary, heavy, stupid, dull, inhuman, vulgar at heart and tiresome in form. I have felt these things so strongly that I have said, 'Ah London, you too then are impossible'. But these are occasional moods; and for one who takes it as I take it, London is on the whole the most possible form of life. I take it as an artist and a bachelor; as one who has the passion of observation and whose business is the study of human life. It is the biggest aggregation of human life – the most complete compendium of the world. The human race is better represented there than anywhere else, and if you learn to know your London, you learn a great many things.

      Henry James, *A Journal*, 1881

※

'It sounds like Shakespeare,' said Walter.

'Well, sir, I understand he portrayed life. And that is what it is.'

'Everything comes into it,' said Julia.

'Yes, ma'am. It is a comprehensive term.'

    Ivy Compton Burnett, *A Heritage and its History*

※

They went quietly down into the roaring streets, inseparable and blessed; and as they passed along in the sunshine and shade, the noisy and the eager, and the arrogant and froward and the vain, fretted and chafed, and made their usual uproar.

    Charles Dickens, last lines of *Little Dorrit*

※

The Catholic solution of our problem, of our unique vital problem, the problem of immortality and eternal salvation of the individual soul, satisfies the will and therefore satisfies life; but the attempts to rationalise it by means of dogmatic theology fail to satisfy the reason. And the reason has its exigencies as imperious as those of life.

Graham Greene in *Ways of Escape,* quoting from Miguel de Unamuno's *Tragic Sense of Life* to describe his distrust of theology

Advice on low spirits

Nobody has suffered more from low spirits than I have done, so I feel for you. 1. Live as well and drink as much wine as you dare. 2. Go into the shower bath with a small quantity of water at a temperature low enough to give you a slight sensation of cold – 75° or 80°. 3. Amusing books. 4. Short views of human life not further than lunch or tea. 5. Be as busy as you can. 6. See as much as you can of friends who respect and like you; 7. and of those acquaintance who amuse you. 8. Make no secret of low spirits to your friends but talk of them fully; they are always the worse for dignified concealment. 9. Attend to the effects tea and coffee produce on you. 10. Compare your lot with that of other people. 11. Don't expect too much of human life, a sorry business at the best. 12. Avoid poetry, dramatic representations (except comedy), music, serious novels, melancholy sentimental people and everything likely to excite feeling or emotion not ending in active benevolence. 13. Do good and endeavour to please everybody of every degree. 14. Be as much as you can in the open air without fatigue. 15. Make the room where you commonly sit gay and pleasant. 16. Struggle little by little against idleness. 17. Don't be too severe on yourself, but do yourself justice. 18. Keep good blazing fires. 19. Be firm and constant in the exercise of rational religion. 20. Believe me, dear Lady Georgiana, truly yours, Sydney Smith.

Sydney Smith to Lady Georgiana Morpeth

∞

> The heights by great men reached and kept
> Were not attained by sudden flight,
> But they, while their companions slept,
> Were toiling upward in the night.

Longfellow, quoted at the beginning of Lord Beaverbrook's *Men and Power 1917-1918*

∞

We jogged back in silence. Apart from one visit to Roger Chetwode this was my first venture outside my family. It seemed likely to end on the evening it began. When we reached the house Lord Birkenhead turned to me. 'We have survived,' he said, 'though you will not, I feel sure, claim an undue share of credit for that achievement. We have preserved our skins, if not our dignity. In reciting these events to the ladies it would be unwise, and indeed, injudicious, to depress their spirits and our own prestige with too slavish an adherence to the literal facts as they may have appeared at the moment of their occurrence.'

He shot me the rich warm illuminating smile of partnership I came to know so well, and went in to pitch some tremendous yarn in which he and I won infinite glory and saved each other's lives.

Frank Longford, *Born to Believe* (Frank Pakenham's pony and Lord Birkenhead's horse had bolted when they went riding together.)

Possessions lost, something lost;
Honour lost, much lost;
Courage lost, everything lost.

> Bernard Levin, quoting Goethe

My mother might not have been a comforting refuge in my childhood nor take much loving interest in me now I was a man, but she had by her example shown me many qualities to admire and value. Professionalism, for instance; a tough minded singleness of purpose; a refusal to be content with a low standard when a higher one could be achieved merely by working … because I saw the grind behind the gloss of her public performances I grew up not expecting life's plums to be tossed into my lap without any effort from me. What mother could teach her son more?

> Dick Francis, *Nerve* (the narrator speaking)

There is never any distress that an hour's reading will not relieve.

> Charles-Louis de Montesquieu

The Woodspurge

The wind flapped loose, the wind was still
Shaken out dead from tree or hill;
I had walked on at the wind's will, –
I sat now, for the wind was still,

Between my knees my forehead was –
My lips, drawn in, said not Alas!
My hair was over in the grass,
My naked ears heard the day pass.

My eyes, wide open, had the run
Of some ten weeds to fix upon;
Among these few, out of the sun,
The woodspurge flowered, three cups in one.

From perfect grief there need not be
Wisdom or even memory;
One thing then learned remains to me, –
The woodspurge has a cup of three.

Dante Gabriel Rossetti

∞

The soul's dark cottage, battered and decayed,
Lets in new light through chinks that time has made.

Edmund Waller, 'Of the Last Verses in the Book'

∞

Conception, my boy, fundamental brain work is what makes all the difference in art.

> Dante Gabriel Rossetti

The Last Wasp

When light dims to an early blur
Which makes me dream I'm going blind,
When the last wasp, colourless fur,
Blends with the carpet; when I find
Soles chilled by linoleum, the moon
Rotten and low, and bonfire smoke
Perplexing the late afternoon
With tears that irrigate and choke;
When mist with mortuary breath
Doodles on windows notes for death

When, with a histrionic sigh
The year turns its face to the wall
Of winter and pretends to die
Then is the time I like to call
Its bluff, and either counter-attack
By rushing into love and work
Or take the long muddy slog back
Through memory. Either way the jerk
Of one or the other blistering rope
Tightens and lifts some flag of hope.

> James Michie

As I have taken such an aversion to the character of Author, I have fallen into a taste that I never had in my life, that of music. The swan, you know, Madam, is drawing towards its end, when it thinks of warbling, but as I have not begun to sing myself, I trust it is but distantly symptomatic. In short, I have only lived with musicians lately and liked them. Mr Jerningham is here at Twickenham, and sings in charming taste to his harp. My niece Miss Churchill has been here with her harp, and plays ten times better and sings worse – but I am quite enchanted with Mr Gammon, the Duke of Grafton's brother-in-law. It is the most melodious voice I ever heard; like Mr Meynell's, but more perfect. As I pass a great deal of time at Hampton Court, in a way very much like the remnant of the Court of St Germain's (– and I assure you, where there are some that I believe were of that Court), I was strolling in the gardens in the evening with my nieces, who joined Lady Schaub and Lady Fitzroy, and the former asked Mr Gammon to sing. His taste is equal to his voice, and his deep notes, the part I prefer, are calculated for the solemnity of Purcell's music, and for what I love particularly, his mad songs and the songs of sailors. It was moonlight and late, and very hot, and the lofty façade of the palace, and the trimmed yews and canal, made me fancy myself of a party in Grammont's time – so you don't wonder that by the help of imagination I never passed an evening more deliciously. When by the aid of some historic vision and local circumstance

I can romance myself into pleasure, nothing transports me so much. Pray, steal from your soldiery, and try this secret at Bevis Mount and Nettley Abbey. There are Lord and Lady Peterborough and Pope to people the former scene, and who you please at Nettley. – I sometimes dream, that one day or other somebody will stroll about poor Strawberry and talk of Lady Ossory – but alas! I am no poet, and my castle is of paper, and my castle and my attachment and I, shall soon vanish and be forgotten altogether!

     Horace Walpole to Lady Ossory, 11 August 1778

∞

No! I am not Prince Hamlet, nor was meant to be;
Am an attendant lord, one that will do
To swell a progress, start a scene or two,
Advise the prince; no doubt an easy tool,
Deferential, glad to be of use,
Politic, cautious and meticulous;
Full of high sentence, but a bit obtuse;
At times, indeed, almost ridiculous,
Almost, at times, the Fool.

    T. S. Eliot, 'The Love Song of J. Alfred Prufrock'

∞

Look not thou on beauty's charming, †
Sit thou still when kings are arming,
Taste not when the wine-cup glistens,

> Speak not when the people listens,
> Stop thy ear against the singer,
> From the red gold keep thy finger,
> Vacant heart and hand and eye,
> Easy live and quiet die.

Walter Scott, *The Bride of Lammermoor*, Lucy Ashton's Song

† Anyone of spirit, as Scott implies, will do the opposite.

∞

L'Apothéose de Lully, 1725, Couperin

Gravement, Lully aux Champs-Elysées concertant avec les ombres lyriques;

Noblement, Descente d'Apollon qui vient offrir son violon à Lully et sa place au Parnasse;

Rondement, Vivement, La Paix du Parnasse…

Played at David Carritt's memorial service, 7 October 1982

∞

Those unhappy people who persuade themselves that intellectual brilliance can in some manner replace the essential virtues of unselfishness, probity, consistency and patience.

Harold Nicolson, *Benjamin Constant*

∞

The productive writer watches the tormented writer as the latter sits down at his desk, chews his fingernails, scratches himself, tears a page to bits, gets up and goes into the kitchen to fix himself a coffee, then reads a poem by Hölderlin (while it is clear to him that Hölderlin has absolutely nothing to do with what he is writing), copies a page already written and then crosses it all out line by line, telephones the cleaners (though it was settled that the blue slacks couldn't be ready before Thursday), then writes some notes that will not be useful now, but maybe later, then goes to the encyclopedia and looks up Tasmania (though it is obvious that in what he is writing there is no reference to Tasmania), tears up two pages, puts on a Ravel recording. The productive writer has never liked the works of the tormented writer; reading them, he always feels as if he is on the verge of grasping a decisive point, but then it eludes him and he is left with a feeling of uneasiness. But now that he is watching him write, he feels this man is struggling with something obscure, a tangle, a road to be dug leading no-one knows where; at times he sees the other man walking on a tight rope stretched over the void and he is filled with admiration.

Italo Calvino, *If On a Winter's Night a Traveller*

∞

Wilberforce's last days

He seems to have found increasing comfort in the thought that he would soon be reunited with all the dear friends who had gone before him. 'I have often heard that sailors on a voyage will drink "friends astern" till they are half way over, then "friends ahead". With me it has been "friends ahead" this long time.'

Robin Birkenhead, *William Wilberforce*

∞

I have never caused anyone to weep. I have never spoken with a haughty voice. I have never made anyone afraid. I have never been deaf to the words of justice and truth.

Egyptian Book of the Dead, quoted by Simone Weil in *Waiting on God*

∞

And so here, O reader, has the time come for us two to part. Toilsome was our journeying together; not without offence; but it is done. To me thou was as a beloved shade, the disembodied or not yet embodied spirit of a brother. To thee I was but as a Voice. Yet was our relation a kind of sacred one; doubt not that! For whatsoever once sacred things become hollow jargons, yet while the Voice of Man speaks with Man, hast thou not there the living fountain out of which all sacredness sprang, and will yet spring? Man, by the nature of him, is definable as 'an incarnated Word'. Ill stands it with me if I have spoken falsely: thine also it was to hear truly. Farewell.

Thomas Carlyle, last lines of *The French Revolution*

'We writers'? Is there any such collective? Doubtless others think so, and suspect us, but I think the opposite is the case: one way of dealing with a temperamental inability to belong to any group whatever.

>P. J. Kavanagh, *Spectator*, 7 April 1984

The reassurance of habit and the priceless gifts of companionship and conversation…

>Richard Cobb, *Death in Paris*

J'étais seul, l'autre soir, au Théâtre Français
Ou presque seul; l'auteur n'avait pas grand succès,
Ce n'était que Molière …

>(He sees a girl in the theatre, and
>recalls a couplet of Andre Chénier)

'Sous votre amiable tête, un cou blanc, délicat,
Se plie, et de la neige effacerait l'éclat.'

>Alfred de Musset, 'Une soirée perdue'

Tristesse

J'ai perdu ma force et ma vie
Et mes amis et ma gaîté;
J'ai perdu jusqu'à la fierté
Qui faisait croire à mon génie.

Quand j'ai connu la Vérité
J'ai cru que c'était une amie;
Quand je l'ai comprise et sentie,
J'en étais déjà degoûté.

Et pourtant elle est éternelle,
Et ceux qui se sont passés d'elle
Ici-bas ont tout ignoré.

Dieu parle, il faut qu'on lui réponde,
Le seul bien qui me reste au monde
Est d'avoir quelquefois pleuré.

Alfred de Musset

∞

Spirits of my unknown ancestors speak through me;
green hills of Staffordshire stand firm in my mind.

John Wain, last lines of *Sprightly Running*

∞

The secret... of making limited opportunities endurable, which she deemed to consist in the cunning enlargement, by a species of microscopic treatment, of those minute forms of satisfaction that offer themselves to anyone not in positive pain, which, thus handled, have much of the same inspiring effect upon life as wider interests cursorily embraced.

Thomas Hardy, The Mayor of Casterbridge

∞

Apple Blossom †

The first blossom was the best blossom
For the youth who had never seen an orchard;
For the youth whom whiskey had led astray
The morning after was the first day.

The first apple was the best apple
For Adam before he heard the sentence;
When the flaming sword endorsed the Fall
The trees were his to plant for all.

The first ocean was the best ocean
For the child from streets of doubt and litter;
For the youth for whom the skies unfurled
His first love was his first world.

But the first verdict seemed the worst verdict
When Adam and Eve were expelled from Eden;
Yet when the bitter gates clanged to
The sky beyond was just as blue.

For the next ocean is the first ocean
And the last ocean is the first ocean
And, however often the sun may rise,
A new thing dawns upon our eyes.

For the last blossom is the first blossom
And the first blossom is the best blossom
And when from Eden we take our way
The morning after is the first day.

Louis MacNeice.

† This poem is the best cure for a broken heart I know.

∞

In whatever form a slowly accumulated past lives in the blood – whether in the concrete image of the old house stored with visual memories or in the conception of the house not built with hands but made up of inherited passions and loyalties – it has the same power of broadening and deepening the individual existence, of attaching it by mysterious links of kinship to all the mighty sum of human striving.

Edith Wharton, *The House of Mirth*

∞

There is an art of the future, and it is going to be so lovely and so young that even if we give up our youth for it we must gain in serenity by it. Perhaps it is very silly to write all this, but I feel it so strongly; it seems to me that, like me, you have been suffering to see your youth pass away like a puff of smoke; but if it grows again, and comes to life in what you make, nothing has been lost and the power to work is another youth.

Vincent van Gogh to his brother Theo

∞

… Look thy last on all things lovely
Every hour; let no night
Seal thy sense in deathly slumber
Till to delight
Thou hast paid thy utmost blessing
Since those things that thou dost praise
Beauty took from those who loved them
In other days.

Walter de la Mare, 'Fare Well'

∞

Fate loves the analogies of what we call chance, and is fond of playing in a mysterious way with figures.

Stefan Zweig, *Marie Antoinette*, explaining how Fersen was killed on 20 June, the same date as the flight to Varennes

∞

The supreme vice is shallowness.

Oscar Wilde, *De Profundis*

∞

Innocent through no fault of my own.

> Günter Grass

∞

Charlie's death has brought home to me to take nothing for granted and to savour friendship.

> Fiona Douglas-Home in a letter about her brother

∞

À chaque jour suffit sa peine.

> Quoted by Marie Noële Kelly

∞

One lesson I have learned in my wandering life, my friends, is never to call anything a misfortune until you have seen the end of it. Is not every hour a fresh point of view?

> Arthur Conan Doyle, *The Exploits of Brigadier Gerard*

∞

> Better by far than gaudy bougainvillea
> Seen from an easy chair in tropic day
> The sight of snowdrops simple and unfrilly are

To winter walkers on the South Downs way.

> Miles Jebb, 'A Winter Journey'

∞

An Irishman, you know, is seldom cast down unless he is going to be hanged, and even then, two to one, he will have a joke with Jack Ketch.

Sir Martin Archer Shee to his friend Constable to cheer him up on having a rheumatic knee

∞

The password is fortitude.

> Violet Needham, *The Black Riders*

∞

Life, we've been long together
Through sunny and through stormy weather
'Tis hard for friends to say goodbye
Perhaps t'will cost a tear, a sigh.
Then steal away, give little warning,
Choose thine own time,
Say not good night but in some brighter clime
Bid me good morning.

Anna Laetitia Barbauld, quoted by Fanny Burney in old age

∞

My grace is sufficient for thee, my strength is made perfect in weakness.

2 Corinthians, 12:9

It is therefore necessary to be suspicious of those who seek to convince us with means other than reason, and of charismatic leaders; we must be cautious about delegating to others our judgement and our will. Since it is difficult to distinguish true prophets from false, it is as well to regard all prophets with suspicion. It is better to renounce revealed truths, even if they exalt us by their splendour or if we find them convenient because we can acquire them gratis. It is better to content oneself with other more modest and less exciting truths, those one acquires painfully, little by little, without shortcuts, those that can be verified and demonstrated.

Primo Levi, Afterword to *If This is a Man/The Truce*

We hardly know life, we know so little of its foundation, and besides, we are living in a period in which everybody seems to be talking nonsense, and everything seems to be in a tottering state, so it cannot be called unhappy if we have found a duty that forces us to remain quietly in our corner, busy with our modest work.

Vincent van Gogh to his sister Wilhelmina

The splendour falls on castle walls
And snowy summits old in story;
The long light shakes across the lakes
And the wild cataract leaps in glory.
Blow, bugle, blow, set the wild echoes flying.
Blow, bugle; answer, echoes, dying, dying, dying.

O hark, O hear! how thin and clear,
And thinner, clearer, farther going!
O sweet and far from cliff and scar
The horns of Elfland faintly blowing!
Blow, let us hear the purple glens replying.
Blow, bugle; answer, echoes, dying, dying, dying.

O love, they die in yon rich sky,
They faint on hill or field or river:
The echoes roll from soul to soul
And grow for ever and for ever.
Blow, bugle, blow, set the wild echoes flying
And answer, echoes, answer, dying, dying, dying.

Alfred, Lord Tennyson, 'The Princess'

People say that Life is the thing, but I prefer reading.

Logan Pearsall Smith, *All Trivia*

Your children are not your children.
They are the sons and daughters of life's longing for itself.
They come through you but not from you,
And though they are with you yet they belong not to you.
You may give them your love but not your thoughts,
For they have their own thoughts.
You may house their bodies but not their souls,
For their souls live in the house of tomorrow which you cannot visit, not even in your dreams.
You may strive to be like them, but seek not to make them like you.
For life goes not backward nor tarries with yesterday.
You are the bows from which your children as living arrows are sent forth,
The archer sees the mark upon the mark of the infinite and he bends you with his might that the arrows may go swift and free.
Let your bending in the archer's hand be for gladness;
For even as He loves the arrow that flies,
He loves also the bow that is stable.

Kahlil Gibran, *The Prophet*

I do not suppose he had any dogmatic and doctrinal opinions in respect to religion… in his heart of hearts he despised and derided all that the world wrangles and squabbles about; but he had the true religion of benevolence and charity, of peace and good will to mankind, which, let us hope (as I firmly believe) to be all sufficient, be the truth of the great mystery what it may.

    Charles Greville on Sydney Smith, hearing of his death

∞

'Even now,' she thought, 'almost no-one remembers Esteban and Pepita but myself. Camilla alone remembers her uncle Pio and her son; this woman her mother. But soon we shall die and the memory of those five will have left the earth, and we ourselves shall be loved for a while and forgotten. But the love will have been enough; all those impulses of love return to the love that made them. Even memory is not necessary for love. There is a land of the living and a land of the dead, and the bridge is love, the only survival, the only meaning.

Thornton Wilder, *The Bridge of San Luis Rey*, remembering those who fell from the bridge of San Luis Rey

∞

'What a strange thing!' said the overseer of the workmen at the foundry. 'This broken lead heart will not melt in the furnace. We must throw it away.' So they threw it on a dustheap where the dead swallow was also lying.

'Bring me the two most precious things in the city,' said God to one of his Angels; and the Angel brought him the leaden heart and the dead bird.

'You have rightly chosen,' said God, 'for in my

Garden of Paradise this little bird shall sing for ever more, and in my city of gold the Happy Prince shall praise me.'

> Oscar Wilde, 'The Happy Prince'

∞

We all lived beside her, and never understood that she was that righteous one without whom, according to the proverb, no village can stand.
 Nor any city.
 Nor our whole land.

> Alexander Solzhenitsyn, *Matryona's House*

∞

I get into bed, turn out the light, say 'bugger the lot of them' and go to sleep.

> Winston Churchill, on getting to sleep in times of stress

∞

All his writing was less than himself. I think it ought always to be disappointing to meet an artist; if his work is not something invisible in him he can't have the real motive for work. Artists are to be heard and not seen.'

> Evelyn Waugh to Diana Cooper, re. Maurice Baring

∞

What I want is to be able to live like a poor man with plenty of money.

Pablo Picasso

English cold and fog and rain, grey twilight among isolated, bare trees and dripping coverts; London streets when the shops were closing and the pavements crowded with people going to the Tube stations with evening papers; empty streets, late at night after dances, revealing unexpected slopes, sluiced by men in almost medieval overalls.

Evelyn Waugh, *Black Mischief*

'Thinking has, many a time, made me sad, darling; but doing never did in all my life. My theory is a sort of parody on the maxim "Get money, my son, honestly if you can; but get money". My precept is "Do something, my sister, do good if you can, but at any rate do something".'

'Not excluding mischief,' said Margaret, smiling faintly through her tears.

'By no means. What I do exclude is the remorse afterwards. Blot your misdeeds out (if you are particularly conscientious), by a good deed, as soon as you can; just as we did a correct sum on the slate at school, where an incorrect one was only half rubbed out. It was better than wetting our sponge with our tears; both less loss of time, where tears had to be waited for, and a better effect at last.'

Mrs Gaskell, *North and South*

∞

He never thought an honour done him
Because a Duke was proud to own him;
Would rather slip aside and choose
To talk with wits in dirty shoes …
He never courted men in station
Nor person had in admiration;
Of no man's goodness was afraid
Because he sought for no man's aid.

Jonathan Swift, 'Verses on the Death of Mr Swift'

∞

They had made a grave error in their summing up of Hastings' character, deceived by his mild appearance and general manner, and the fact that till then he seemed to lack any real fire in his own defence. They were unaware of an inner courage, a doggedness to persevere, invariably fortified by adversity. Not for a moment did they suspect that their intended victim was capable of a ruthlessness which could outrival their own, and infinitely more dangerous in that it lay concealed beneath a normally urbane exterior.

Patrick Turnbull, *Warren Hastings*

∞

It is not that I don't feel and believe in the mystic life, but that I do love the world and feel that there is a time for all things and that, while we have mortality, we may as well enjoy it. At the same time I am never unaware of its relative smallness in the general picture. The world seems to me like one of those walled gardens full of happy things where one can sit and look through the little windows of the wall to the expanses of Reality. And why hurry so much to get out into those spaces? Sufficient to know them there and that we shall be taken there in good time.

> Freya Stark to Sydney Cockerell, 27 August 1956

∞

Wishes for the Months

I wish you in January, the swirl of blown snow –
A green January makes a full churchyard;

Thrushes singing through the February rain; in March
The clarion winds, the daffodils;

April, capricious as an adolescent girl,
With cuckoo song and cuckoo flowers;

May with a dog rose, June with a musk rose; July
Multi-foliate, with all the flowers of summer;

August – a bench in the shade and a cool tankard;
September golden among his sheaves;

In October, apples; in grave November
Offerings for the beloved dead;

And in December, a mid-winter stillness.
Promise of a new life, incarnation.

John Heath Stubbs

∞

And slowly answered Arthur from the barge:
'The old order changeth, yielding place to new,
And God fulfils Himself in many ways,
Lest one good custom should corrupt the world.
Comfort thyself, what comfort is in me?
I have lived my life, and that which I have done
May He within Himself make pure! but thou
If thou shouldst never see my face again,
Pray for my soul. More things are wrought by prayer
Than this world dreams of ...'

Alfred, Lord Tennyson, *Morte d'Arthur*

∞

'I don't see that,' he said, as we crossed Piccadilly Circus. 'In actual life it isn't so. What is there to prevent a motor-omnibus from knocking me over and killing me at this moment?'

At that moment, by what has always seemed to me the strangest of co-incidences and just the kind of thing that playwrights ought to avoid, a motor-omnibus knocked Brown over and killed him.

Max Beerbohm, 'Savonarola Brown'

∞

Wheresoever your life endeth there is it all. The profit of life consists not in the space, but rather in the use. Some have lived long who have lived but a short while. Make use of life while you have it. Whether you have lived enough depends on yourself, not on the human measure of your years. Did you imagine you would never arrive at the place towards which you were forever moving? There is no road but has an end. And if company may solace you, doth not the whole world go the same way?

Michel de Montaigne

∞

Petrella went out into streets which were pearly grey with mist. It was the pleasant mist of early November, which comes up from the river after a warm autumn day and bears no resemblance to the same London fog which rolls in late in the year, from the North Sea, saturated with filth and sends Londoners coughing and choking to their twilight homes.

This mist was a feathery outrider of winter, with

implications of football, open fires and hot toast, a fairy godmother of the good natured type, who veiled all the street lamps in gauze, softened the angular austerities of brick and slate, and doubled the attraction of the little red curtained windows of pubs.

Michael Gilbert, *Blood and Judgement*

He who would do good to another must do it in Minute Particulars… General Good is the plea of the scoundrel, hypocrite and flatterer… For Art and Science cannot exist but in minutely organised particulars.

William Blake

Afterwards

When the Present has latched its postern behind my tremulous stay,
And the May month flaps its glad green leaves like wings,
Delicate-filmed as new-spun silk, will the neighbours say,
'He was a man who used to notice such things'?

If it be in the dust when, like an eyelid's soundless blink,
The dew-fall hawk comes crossing the shades to alight
Upon the wind-warped upland thorn, a gazer may think
'To him this must have been a familiar sight.'

If I pass during some nocturnal blackness, mothy and warm,
When the hedgehog travels furtively over the lawn,

One may say, 'He strove that innocent creatures should come to no harm,
But he could do little for them; and now he is gone.'

If, when hearing that I have been stilled at last, they stand at the door,
Watching the full-starred heavens that winter sees,
Will this thought rise on those who will meet my face no more,
'He was one who had an eye for such mysteries'?

And will any say when my bell of quittance is heard in the gloom,
And a crossing breeze cuts a pause in its out-rollings,
Till they rise again, as they were a new bell's bloom
'He hears it not now, but used to notice such things'?

Thomas Hardy

∞

The telephone rang. My intuition suggests a wrong number. Not that great intuition is needed; a nearby new cinema has been granted a number that is only one digit away from mine, and wrong numbers are common. This is one.

'Can you tell me the time of the last complete show?'
'You have the wrong number.'
'Eh? Is that the Odeon?'
I decide to give a Burtonian answer.
'No, this is the Great Theatre of Life. Admission is free but the taxation is mortal. You come when you can and leave when you must. The show is continuous. Good night.'

Robertson Davies, *The Cunning Man*

He had learnt that having someone to care for is the same as being cared for oneself.

>J. C. Ballard, *Empire of the Sun*

Mr Wodehouse's idyllic world can never stale. He will continue to release future generations from a captivity that may be more irksome than our own. He has created a world for us to live and delight in.

>Evelyn Waugh, re P. G. Wodehouse

Fantaisies d'hiver

Dans le bassin des Tuileries,
Le cygne s'est pris en nageant
Et les arbres, comme au féeries
Sont en filigrane d'argent.

Les vases ont des fleurs de givre,
Sous la charmille au blancs réseaux;
Et sur la neige on voit se suivre
Les pas étoilés des oiseaux.

Au piedestal ou, court-vêtue,
Venus coudoyait Phocion,

L'Hiver a posé pour statue
La Frileuse de Clodion.

> Théophile Gautier

∞

Epitaphum Felis

By weight of the wearying years, and by grievous illness
Compelled, I come at last to the Lethean lakes-side;
'Have thou Elysian suns,' said Prosperina smiling,
   'Elysian meadows'.
Nay, but if I deserve it, O kindly Queen of the silence,
Grant me this boon, one night to return to the homestead,
Home to return by night, and into the master's ear,
Whisper, Across the waste of the Stygian waters
Your Felis, most faithful of cats, still holds you dear.

> John Jortin, 18th century, translated by Seamus O'Sullivan

∞

We who write today and whose work may be totally forgotten in a hundred years' time should not be discouraged. Some of us will live and the rest will have made a contribution. We have been part of the Zeitgeist, and unless there is a firm foundation of literate writing, and pool of ideas in which to dip, those few, those very few, who are going to scale the heights would never have been able to start.

> Author unknown, *Essays by Divers Hands*

∞

All is over: brief career,
Dash of greyhounds slipping thongs,
Flash of falcon, leap of deer,
Cold air rushing up the lungs,
Sound of many tongues.
We tarry on; we're toiling still;
He's gone and he fares the best,
He fought against the odds and up the hill;
He has earned his rest.

Author unknown, quoted by Winston Churchill, and used by his secretary Jock Colville as the finis to his memoir of Churchill, *Footprints in Time*.

∞

Having complained of frantic novels, sickly and stupid German tragedies, idle and extravagant stories in verse, and the degrading thirst after outrageous stimulation (a feast for any Minister of Culture), Wordsworth concluded with a muted but indispensable flourish of trumpets: 'Reflecting upon the magnitude of the general evil, I should be oppressed with no dishonourable melancholy, had I not a deep impression of certain inherent and indestructible qualities of the human mind.'

D. J. Enright, *Injury Time*

∞

The Last Laugh

I made hay while the sun shone.
My work sold.
Now, if the harvest is over
And the world cold;
Give me the bonus of laughter
As I lose hold.

John Betjeman, quoted in *The Bonus of Laughter* by Alan Pryce Jones

∞

I am old. Nothing interests me now,
Moreover I am not very intelligent,
And my ideas have travelled no further
Than my feet. You ask me
What is the greatest happiness on earth?
It is to hear a young girl
Singing along the road
After she has asked you the way.

Wang Wei (thirteenth century)

∞

It is art that makes life, makes interest, makes importance, for our consideration and appreciation of these things, and I know of no substitute whatever for its force and power.

Henry James to H. G. Wells

How Winter came in the Lake Region

That night I felt the winter in my veins,
A joyous tremor of the icy glow;
And woke to hear the north's wild vibrant strains
While far and wide by withered woods and plains
Fast fell the driving snow.

Wilfred Campbell, quoted in Robertson Davies, *The Merry Heart*

It is not growing like a tree
In bulk, doth make men better be;
Or standing long an oak, three hundred year
To fall a log at last, dry, cold and sear:
A lily of the day
Is fairer far in May,
Although it fall and die that night
It was the plant and flower of light.
In small proportions we just beauties see;
And in short measures, life may perfect be.

Ben Jonson, 'A part of an Ode'

Beyond Decoration

Stalled, in the middle of a rented room,
The couple who own it quarrelling in the yard
Outside, about which shade of Snowcem
They should use. (From my bed I'd heard
Her say she liked me in my dressing gown
And heard her husband's grunt of irritation.
Some ladies like sad men who are alone.)
But I am stalled, and sad is not the word.
Go out I cannot, nor can I stay in,
Becalmed, mid carpet, breathless, on the road
To nowhere and the road has petered out.
This was twenty years ago and bad as that.
I must have moved at last, for I knelt down,
Which I had not before, nor thought I should,
It would not be exact to say I prayed;
What for? The one I wanted there was dead.
All I could do was kneel and so I did.
At once I entered dark so vast and warm
I wondered it could fit inside the room
When I looked round. The road I had to walk down
Was still there. From that moment it was mean
Beyond my strength to doubt what I had seen:
A heat at the heart of dark, so plainly shown,
A bowl, of two cupped hands, in which a pain
That filled the room could be engulfed and drown
And yet, for truth is in the bowl, remain ...
Today I thought it time to write this down,
Beyond decoration, humble, in plain rhyme,
As clear as I could, and as truthful, which I have done.

                         P. J. Kavanagh, *Collected Poems*

Extreme friendliness amounts to condescension.

James Lees Milne

All nice rooms are a bit shabby.

Nancy Mitford

Gloom is no Christian temper. We must live in the sunshine even when we sorrow.

Cardinal Newman

You make a living by what you get. You make a life by what you give.

Winston Churchill

> Else I myself should much mistake
> To harbour a divided thought
> From all my kind that for my sake
> There should a miracle be wrought.

No, I do know that I was born
    For age, misfortune, sickness, grief,
But I will bear them with such scorn
    As shall not need thy false relief.

Nor for my part shall I go far,
    As wanderers do that still may roam
But make my strengths such as they are
    Here in my bosom and at home.

Ben Jonson, 'The Forest'

A journalist once asked her to define 'good behaviour' [the name of her best-known novel] and she gave a considered reply: 'Never telling all, keeping a smiling face when things are going against you, consideration, good manners, punctuality, never boasting.'

From the obituary of Molly Keane, *Daily Telegraph*

Even Mr March, the most realistic of men, could not always forgive himself for his own nature. He could not quite forget the illusion which we all have, most strongly when we are young, that every kind of action is possible to us if only we use our will. He felt, as we all do, when we have to come to terms with our temperament and no longer try to be different from ourselves, we may be happier now but we cannot help looking back to the days when we struggled against the sight of our limitations, when miserable and conflict-ridden perhaps, we still had flashes of hope we held the whole world in our hands. For the loss, as we come to know ourselves, is that we now know what we can never do.

C. P. Snow, *The Conscience of the Rich*

∞

It was that prolonged, flat, cheerless week that follows Christmas. My own existence seemed infinitely stagnant, relieved only by work on another book. Those interminable latter days of the dying year create an interval, as it were, of moral suspension: one form of life already passed away before another has had time to assert some new endemic characteristic. Imminent change of direction is for some reason often foreshadowed by such colourless patches of time.

Anthony Powell, *The Acceptance World*

∞

Who, going through the vale of misery, use it for a well.

Psalm 84:6. Quoted by David Cairns in *Mozart and his Operas*

∞

Hope that the way is long
That the summer evenings are many,

When you enter at last, with such joy
Ports that you are seeing for the first time;
May you stop at Phoenician markets
And purchase fine goods,
Mother of pearl and coral and amber and ebony,
And sensual perfumes of every kind,
As many sensual perfumes as you can.
And may you visit many Egyptian cities
To learn and learn from their scholars,
Always keep Ithaca in your mind,
To arrive there is your destiny
But do not hurry the journey in any way.
Better that it should last for many years.

    Constantin Cavafy, 'Ithaca', translator unknown

∞

A father and a mother ought to mean more to each other than the children do. If they live only for their children, the children don't get a chance to live themselves.

    G. B. Edwards, *The Book of Ebenezer Le Page*

∞

How the snow weighs down the branches
and the years stoop the shoulders so dear;
the years of youth are far-away years.

Japanese poem quoted in *The Paper Moon* by Andrea Camilleri, translated by Stephen Sartarelli

In every serious undertaking there comes a moment when only honour and determination keep one going.

G. K. Chesterton

There are certain scenes that (far more than artefacts dug up out of the ground or prehistoric paintings, which have a confusing freshness or newness) serve to remind us of how old the human race is and of the beautiful touching sameness of most human occasions. Anything that is not anonymous is a dream. And who we are, and whether our parents embraced life or were disappointed by it, and what will become of our children couldn't be less important. Nobody asks the name of the athlete tying his sandal on the curved side of the Greek vase or whether the traveller on the Chinese scroll arrived at the inn before dark.

William Maxwell, *The Chateau*

There is always the danger that people who work hard become blinded by the work itself, and by a paradox, lazy minded.

V. S. Pritchett, *The Midnight Oil*

An experience that surely enhances the quality of the lives of those who see it, and which provides, as great art sometimes does – indeed, I sometimes think it is art's chief function – that secret well of joy at which we can drink forever.

Bernard Levin re. Eduardo de Filippo's *Saturday, Sunday, Monday*

∞

Still glides the stream, and shall forever glide,
The form remains, the Function never dies;
While we, the brave, the mighty and the wise,
We Men who in our pride of youth defied
The elements, must vanish, be it so!
Enough if something from our hands have power
To live, and act, and serve the future hour;
And if, as tow'rd the silent tomb we go,
Thro' love, thro' hope and faith's transcendent dower,
We feel that we are greater than we know.

William Wordsworth, conclusion to 'The River Duddon'

∞

What about the creative state? In it a man is taken out of himself. He lets down as it were a bucket into the subconscious and draws up something which is obviously beyond his reach. He mixes this thing with his normal experience and out of this mixture he makes a work of art. And when the process is over, when the picture or symphony or lyric or novel (or whatever it is) is complete the artist looking back on it, will wonder how on earth he did it. And indeed he did not do it on earth.

> E. M. Forster, *Aspects of the Novel*

∞

> Nous naissons, nous vivons, bergère,
> Nous mourons sans savoir comment;
> Chacun est parti du néant:
> Où va-t-il … Dieu le sait, ma chère.

> Voltaire, 'À Madame Lullin', written at the age of 80

∞

A Library

> New books each year
> Meet old books here
> And new books too
> Old eyes renew;
> So youth and age
> Like ink and page
> In this house join,
> Minting new coin.
>
> Philip Larkin

∞

Wine haiku

A perfect white wine
is sharp, sweet and cold as this:
birdsong in winter.

Wendy Cope

∞

But to have done, instead of not doing
this is not vanity …
To have gathered from the air a live tradition
or from a fine old eye the unconquered flame.
This is not vanity.
Here error is all in the not done.
All in the diffidence that faltered.

Ezra Pound, ending of Canto LXXXI, quoted in talk by Stoddard Martin

∞

Que ma saison dernière
Soit encore le printemps.

Jean de Béranger

∞

I was thinking that I would never believe anyone who told me that life – with all it contained of love, and of longing for truth and for happiness, with its summer lightning and the distant sound of water in the night – that it could be without reason or meaning. I would strive to assert its meaning always and everywhere for as long as I lived.

Konstantin Paustovsky, *Story of a Life*

And I think over again
My small adventures
When with a shore wind I drifted out
In my kayak
And thought I was in danger.
My fears
These small ones
That I thought so big,
For all the vital things
I had to get and had to reach.
And yet there is only
One great thing.
The only thing.
To live to see in huts and on journeys
The great day that dawns
And the light that fills the world.

Eskimo poem, seen on a postcard, source unknown

I've been playing for power and position – you can't live that way and remain creative.

Stefan Heym, *The Architects*

Freud has it all wrong: what dominates human beings is this fear of being left alone and it comes from the long helplessness of human childhood when to be abandoned means death.

Sarah Gainham, *Night Falls on the City*

To watch him fumbling with our rich and delicate language is like seeing a Sèvres vase in the hands of a chimpanzee.

Evelyn Waugh on Stephen Spender

It is the greatest mistake of all to do nothing because you can do little. Do what you can.

Sydney Smith

The great characters of fiction live as truly as the memories of great men. For the life after death it is not necessary that a man or woman should have lived.

Samuel Butler, *Notebook*

Unexpected

I drove north that December without expectations;
behind me the old year narrowed into dark lanes of
    disappointment.
At Penrith the night sky threw a constellation of snow
    against my windscreen;
The Whinlatter Pass was closed because of ice.
When I stepped into the lightness of a paneled hall,
you – my friend's sister – greeted me like a hero.

Three years later we married.
The windowsills of the ancient, scarcely used church
standing solitary in the field
brimmed with flowers.
And I sometimes think of those who came later that
afternoon –
unlatching the door, expecting
bare stone and dampness,
and stepping instead into a dream
of scent and white blossom.

                              Anthony Gardner

Fiction has nothing more wild, touching and heart strengthening to place above it.

    G. H. Lewes on Mrs Gaskell's *Life of Charlotte Brontë*

In life one learns that prizes don't always go to the ablest or the ones who were right; they go to the people who are better connected or have the ears of the powers that be. It's stupid to be disappointed.

Julian Amery in *The Oldie*

∞

The longer you look at the paintings the more heavenly they become. They have a sort of early May morning freshness about them and the people all seem as if you watch them a moment more they will complete the gestures they are making.

Diana Athill, *A Florence Diary*, at the Museo di San Marco

∞

There is no-one, however wise, who has not at some period of his youth said things, or lived a life, the memory of which is so unpleasant to him that he would gladly expunge it. And yet he ought not entirely to regret it because he cannot indeed be certain that he has indeed become a wise man – so far as it is possible for any of us to be wise – unless he had passed through all the fatuous and troublesome incarnations by which the ultimate stage must be preceded. I know that there are young people, the sons and grandsons of distinguished men, whose masters have instilled into them nobility of mind and moral refinement from their schooldays. They may perhaps have nothing to retract from their past lives; they could publish a signed account of everything they have ever said or done, but they are poor creatures, feeble descendants of doctrinaires and their wisdom is negative and sterile. We do not receive wisdom, we must discover it ourselves, after a journey through the wilderness which no-one else can make for us, no-one can spare us.

The painter Elstir, in Proust's *Within a Budding Grove*, translated by C. K. Scott-Moncrieff & Terence Kilmartin

∞

> Someone will forever be surprising
> A hunger in himself to be more serious.

Philip Larkin, 'Church Going'

∞

At any gathering I always feel as though I am the youngest person in the room.

W. H. Auden

∞

> … Je voudrais qu'à cet âge,
> On sortît de la vie ainsi que d'un banquet,
> Remerciant son hôte …

Jean de La Fontaine, 'La Mort et le Mourant'

∞

Much better not.

Favourite maxim of the 7th Duke of Devonshire (1808-91)

Acknowledgements

Louis MacNiece: 'Apple Blossom', *Collected Poems*, Faber & Faber

James Michie: 'The Last Wasp', *Collected Poems*, Sinclair-Stevenson

Johh Heath Stubbs: 'Wishes for the Months', *Collected Poems 1943-87*, Carcanet Press

Patrick Kavanagh: 'Beyond Decoration', *Collected Poems*, Carcanet Press

The illustration on page 71 is 'Campanula' by Rosanna Gardner. The cover incorporates a detail from an engraving of 'The House of Cards', after Chardin.

Royalties from this book will go to SANE

http://www.sane.org.uk

SANE